PRAIRIE BOY

FRANK LLOYD WRIGHT TURNS THE HEARTLAND INTO A HOME

BARB ROSENSTOCK

ART BY
CHRISTOPHER SILAS NEAL

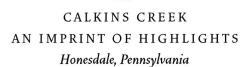

CALKINS CREEK
AN IMPRINT OF HIGHLIGHTS
Honesdale, Pennsylvania

FOR MY FATHER, THE BUILDER

    —BR

FOR MICHAEL SIGNORELLA

    —CSN

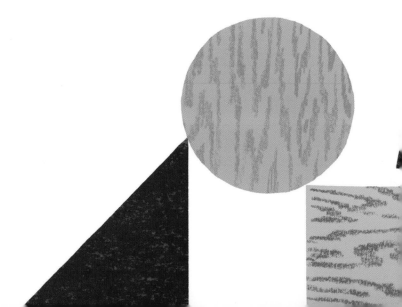

BUILDINGS, TOO,
ARE CHILDREN OF EARTH AND SUN.
—FRANK LLOYD WRIGHT

FRANK WRIGHT TOOK HIS FIRST BREATH ON THE WISCONSIN PRAIRIE. He crawled in the paths of brush-footed butterflies and toddled through waves of tall grass. He skipped past oval milkweed seeds, six-sided honeycombs, and triangle-faced badgers, growing into the kind of boy who wondered . . .

HOW DO BROWN FIELD ANTS
   HIDE IN WHITE QUEEN ANNE'S LACE?

WHEN DOES THE HARVEST MOON
   CHANGE SHAPE?

WHAT MAKES THE PRAIRIE
   FEEL LIKE HOME?

When Frank's father needed work, the family moved from Wisconsin, then moved again—five times in seven years. Frank wound up near the rocky coast of Massachusetts, looking out at gray skies, gray houses, and gray people—turning nine years old with a heart still aching for the shapes of the heartland.

To cheer him up, Frank's mother brought him a gift—
a smooth maple box. He slid off the cover and found three
plain wood blocks:

A SPHERE,

A CUBE,

AND A CYLINDER.

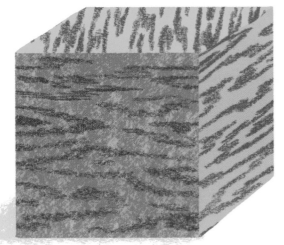

UNDER THE BLOCKS LAY A
SET OF DOWEL RODS

AND THREE LENGTHS OF
ORDINARY STRING.

Frank set up the rods like a mast and hung the blocks from strings.
He spun the blocks, first slow, then fast, and faster still.

Like magic, the spinning cube changed to a cylinder, the spinning cylinder changed to a sphere, and Frank understood that all shapes are connected in ways that made his head spin too.

More blocks from Mother. Rectangles. Triangles. Half-moons. Frank set these new shapes on paper grids, studied sample pictures of pinwheels, crosses, and stars. He shifted one shape to the next, turning piece by piece, his mind like a kaleidoscope. His fingertips memorized smooth faces and sharp edges until the shapes felt like home.

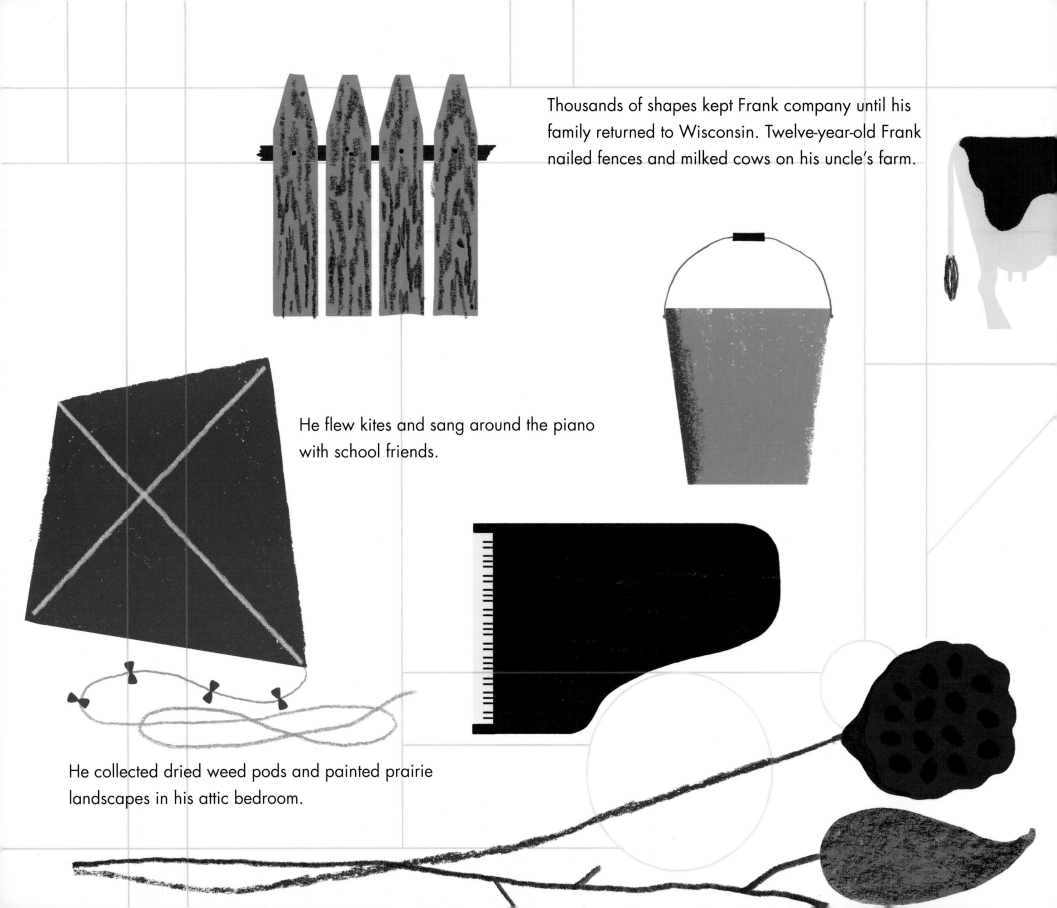

Thousands of shapes kept Frank company until his family returned to Wisconsin. Twelve-year-old Frank nailed fences and milked cows on his uncle's farm.

He flew kites and sang around the piano with school friends.

He collected dried weed pods and painted prairie landscapes in his attic bedroom.

As a teenager, Frank built big dreams. He wanted to draw and think about shapes all the time. He wanted to be an architect.

Frank moved to Chicago, the prairie's biggest city, where buildings grew like wild oats. He spent six years learning from famous architects, sketching detailed plans for the expensive houses they designed.

JASPER CO.
PENCIL FACTORY
RIVER & LEIGH
FURNITURE CO.
ADLER & SULLIVAN
ARCHITECTS
PRINTING

He watched rows of fancy houses go up on flat prairie lots:
Greek Revival, Victorian, Romanesque, Italianate. Houses
shaped like Irish castles built next to houses shaped like
French churches.

Everyone thought these houses were beautiful.
Everyone except Frank.

He thought those fashionable houses stuck out like whales in a wheat field. Frank wondered what made the outsides look crowded. Was it the turrets, finials, and dormers? Or the yellow, green, and blue paint? Frank wondered what made the insides look cramped. Was it the overdressed windows that shut out the sun? Or the boxy rooms stuffed upstairs and down?

To Frank, the old European-style houses didn't fit America's landscape. Families were changing. Household inventions like washers, vacuums, and electric lights meant families had more time for fun!

Frank wondered. What if he designed a new kind of house to fit this new American family?

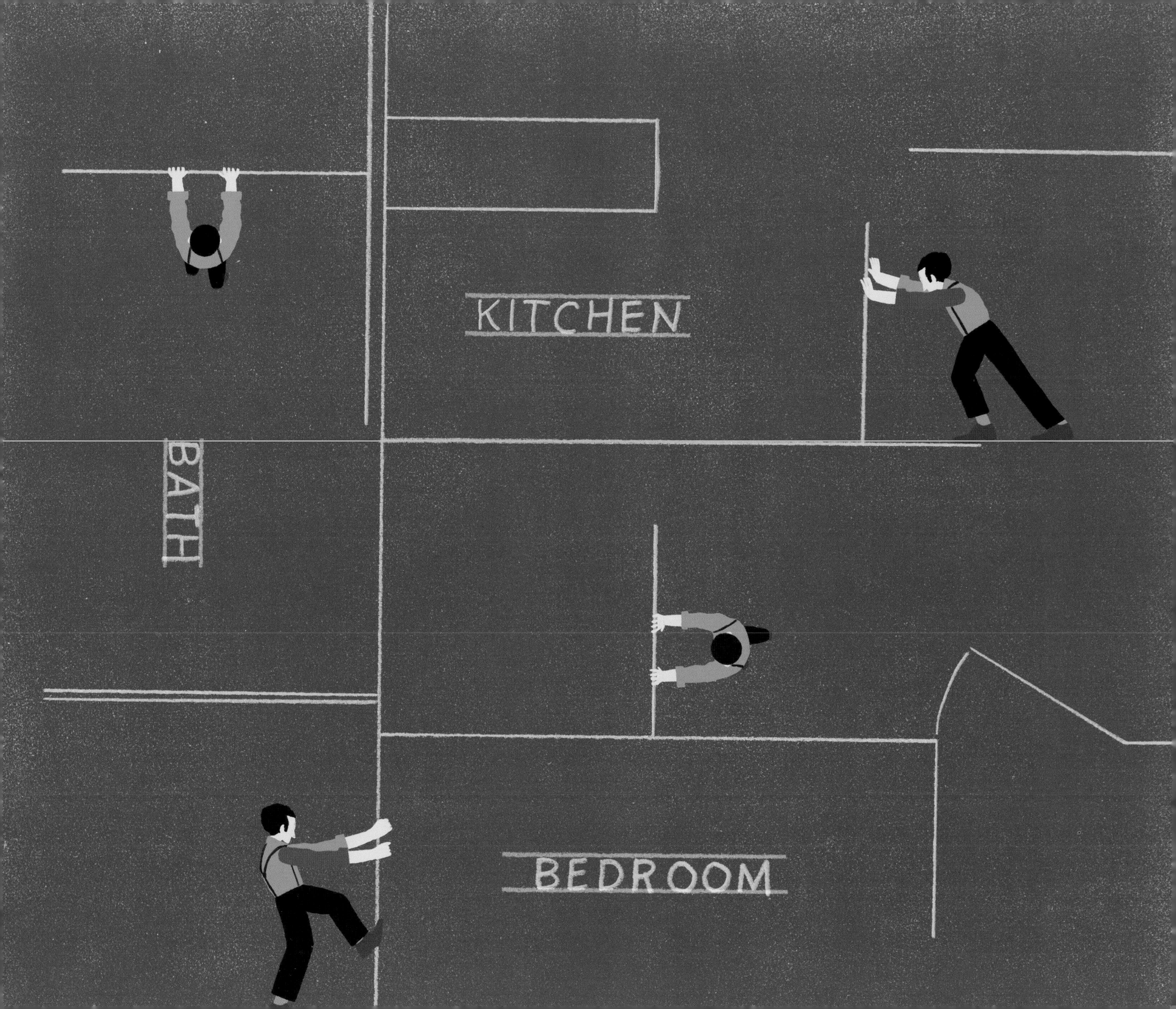
KITCHEN
BATH
BEDROOM

He left his good job, and opened his own office: "FRANK LLOYD WRIGHT, ARCHITECT." There, he let the prairie's shapes tumble from his fingertips.

He sketched long, rectangular houses that snuggled into the flat plains. He colored them in reds, browns, and golds. He hid the front doors from the street, making the houses' vertical lines disappear by coloring mortar to match the brick.

He created banks of windows that let in waves of light, designed winding paths to follow, and built wide, cozy hearths where families laughed together.

Frank Lloyd Wright turned architecture inside out!
He designed HOUSES,

FURNITURE,

sometimes even matching CLOTHES.

Like magic, he shook dozens of shapes from his shirtsleeves—ovals, hexagons, triangles, cubes, spheres, and cylinders.

In Frank's houses people stood on shapes,
sat on shapes,
slept on shapes.
They looked through shapes,
ate off shapes,
played by shape-light.
Frank's buildings grew naturally—
like children, like grasses, like the earth itself.

He called them Prairie Houses . . .
. . . and spun the shapes he loved
into America's home.

Every great architect is—necessarily—a great poet. He must be a great original interpreter of his time, his day, his age.

—Frank Lloyd Wright

AUTHOR'S NOTE

Frank *Lincoln* Wright was born in Richland Center, Wisconsin, on June 8, 1867. His father, William Carey Wright, was a preacher and music teacher from Massachusetts, and his mother, Anna Lloyd Jones, was a teacher from a large Welsh family in Spring Green, Wisconsin. William was widowed with three children (ages ten, eight, and six) when he met Anna. Frank was his mother's favorite child, though he also had two younger sisters. His restless father moved the family frequently to towns in Wisconsin, Iowa, Rhode Island, and Massachusetts. Mrs. Wright learned of Friedrich Froebel's newly invented kindergarten materials (which Froebel called "gifts") at Philadelphia's World's Fair in 1876. Wright credited the various sets of Froebel blocks (and his mother's encouragement) with inspiring his architectural career.

When his parents divorced in 1885, Wright replaced his middle name with Lloyd, his mother's family name. After high school, Wright worked and attended scattered classes at the University of Wisconsin. At nineteen, Frank ran off to Chicago, where he became an apprentice draftsman with Joseph L. Silsbee, a well-known builder of homes, before being hired by the architectural firm Adler & Sullivan. Dankmar Adler was a brilliant engineer, and Louis Sullivan, a groundbreaking architect; their firm helped rebuild Chicago after the Great Fire of 1871. Adler & Sullivan designed homes, theaters, offices, and some of the world's earliest skyscrapers. Wright was hired as a draftsman in 1888, but soon became Sullivan's chief assistant, trusted with creating the final drawings that brought Sullivan's intricate, nature-inspired designs to life.

While working for Adler & Sullivan, Wright began building homes for clients on his own time. In 1893, Wright argued with Sullivan over this freelance work, quit, and opened his own office in Chicago. Frank Lloyd Wright's love of nature, commitment to American democracy, and experiences at other architecture firms resulted in his creation of the first uniquely American homes.

The "Prairie Houses" took their shapes from the landscape and plants. Wright designed leaded glass "light screens," and decorative objects based on the natural shapes of plant forms. He believed in designing in harmony with people and the environment. Open floor plans, one room with many uses, and walls of glass doors and windows are just a few of the influences Wright's prairie homes still have on today's buildings.

As his reputation grew, Wright also designed hotels, churches, shops, stables, skyscrapers, civic centers, colleges, and museums. He believed that beautiful design should be available for all people, not just the rich. He developed a philosophy of "organic architecture" and started an apprenticeship for young architects—first at his Spring Green, Wisconsin, home, called Taliesin (a Welsh word meaning "shining brow," since the house sat on a hillside), and later at Taliesin West, in Scottsdale, Arizona.

Frank Lloyd Wright's buildings stand in thirty-six U.S. states, as well as in Canada and Japan. He designed twelve of the structures listed in *Architectural Record*'s "100 most important buildings of the century"— more than any other architect. Four of his structures made the top ten: Fallingwater (#1), Robie House (#3), Johnson Administration Building (#9), and Unity Temple (#10). Other famous Wright buildings include the Guggenheim Museum in New York and the Hollyhock House in Los Angeles. In 1991, the American Institute of Architects named Wright "the greatest American architect of all time."

In 2015, the Department of the Interior named ten of Wright's projects for consideration as UNESCO World Heritage Sites, places of "Outstanding Universal Value." This marks the first time the U.S. has nominated any of its modern architecture to be protected as "the priceless and irreplaceable assets . . . of humanity as a whole."

No matter how famous he became, Frank Lloyd Wright continued to spend every summer of his long life on the Wisconsin prairie. Its shapes were the ground on which this prairie boy built his revolutionary architecture.

(*Left*) Frank as a young boy
(*Below*) A set of Froebel blocks

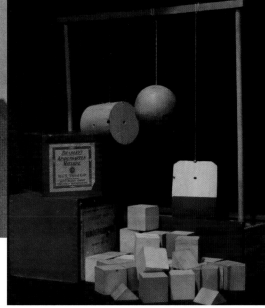

Architect Frank Lloyd Wright
at a drafting table in 1924

SELECTED SOURCES

Brosterman, Norman. *Inventing Kindergarten*. New York: Harry N. Abrams, 1997.

DeLong, David G., curator. *Frank Lloyd Wright: Designs for an American Landscape, 1922–1932*. Library of Congress. Online exhibition. loc.gov/exhibits/flw.

Frank Lloyd Wright Foundation. franklloydwright.org.

Gill, Brendan. *Many Masks: A Life of Frank Lloyd Wright*. New York: G.P. Putnam's Sons, 1987.

Kaufmann, Edgar Jr. "Frank Lloyd Wright's Mementos of Childhood." *Journal of the Society of Architectural Historians*, 11.3 (October 1982): 232–37.

Kieckhefer, Jan. Froebel Block Workshop. Frank Lloyd Wright Trust. Unity Temple, Oak Park, Illinois. June 16, 2014.

Manson, Grant, *Wright in the Nursery*, *The Architectural Review, 113* (June 1953), 349–51.

Secrest, Meryle. *Frank Lloyd Wright*. Chicago: The University of Chicago Press, 1998.

Steffensen, Ingrid. "Frank Lloyd Wright and the 'Gift' of Genius." *The Journal of American Culture* 32.3: 257–66.

Tafel, Edgar. *About Wright: An Album of Recollections by Those Who Knew Frank Lloyd Wright*. New York: John Wiley & Sons, 1993.

Twombly, Robert C. *Frank Lloyd Wright, His Life and His Architecture*. New York: Wiley, 1979.

Wilson, Stuart. "The 'Gifts' of Friedrich Froebel." *Journal of the Society of Architectural Historians* 26.4 (Dec. 1967): 238–41.

Wright, Frank Lloyd. *An Autobiography*. Scottsdale, AZ: Frank Lloyd Wright Foundation, 1943. Reprinted by Barnes & Noble, 1998.

SOURCE NOTES

"Study nature . . ." back cover, Wright, Olgivanna Lloyd, *Frank Lloyd Wright: His Life, His Work, His Words*, New York: Horizon Press, 1966, p. 15.

"Buildings, too . . ." *Architectural Record*, Vol. 62, New York: McGraw-Hill, 1927, p. 322.

"Every great architect . . ." Pfeiffer, Bruce & Nordland, Gerald, *Frank Lloyd Wright in the Realm of Ideas*, Carbondale, IL, Southern Illinois University Press, p. 83.

"gifts . . ." *Inventing Kindergarten*, p. 138.

"Prairie Houses" Wright, p. 132.

"light screens" Wright, p. 142.

"organic architecture" Wright, p. 158.

"shining brow" Wright, p. 167.

"100 most important . . ." *Architectural Record*, July 1991, Vol. 179, McGraw Hill, p. 134–165.

"the greatest American . . ." *FLW Quarterly*, Winter 1992, Vol. 3(1), FLW Foundation, Scottsdale, AZ.

"Outstanding Universal Value" whc.unesco.org/en/criteria/.

"the priceless and irreplaceable . . ." whc.unesco.org/archive/out/guide97.htm.

Fallingwater, Mill Run, Pennsylvania

Robie House, Chicago, Illinois

Frank Lloyd Wright's Architectural Masterpieces Across America

Hollyhock House, Los Angeles, California

Unity Temple, Oak Park, Illinois

Johnson Administration Building, Racine, Wisconsin

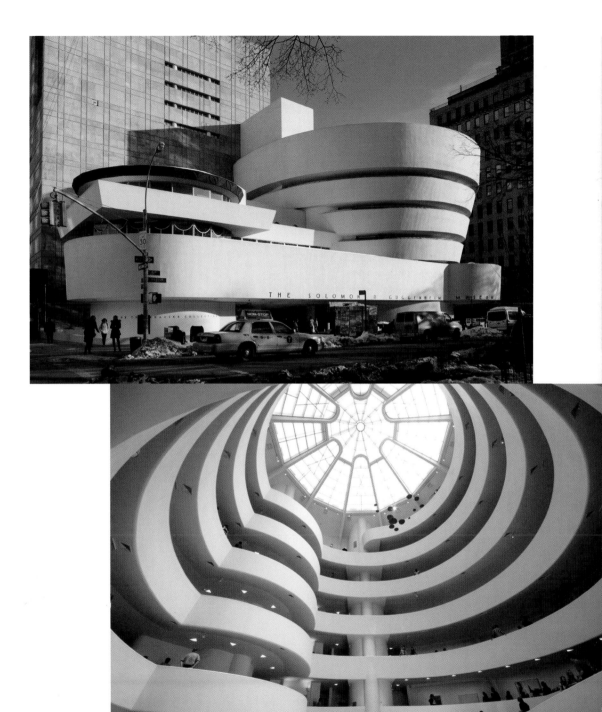

Guggenheim Museum, New York City

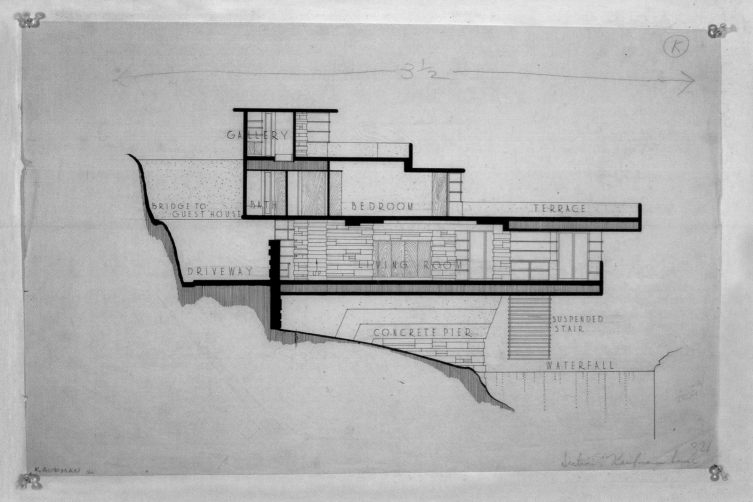

Plans for Fallingwater

ACKNOWLEDGMENTS

My thanks to Margo Stipe, Director and Curator of Collections at the Frank Lloyd Wright Foundation, for her careful reading of this manuscript; and to Jan Kieckhefer, former Director of Education at the Frank Lloyd Wright Preservation Trust, for her detailed explanation of the shapes that influenced Frank Lloyd Wright.

For information about permission to reproduce selections from this book, please contact permissions@highlights.com.

Calkins Creek
An Imprint of Highlights
815 Church Street
Honesdale, Pennsylvania 18431
calkinscreekbooks.com
Printed in China

ISBN: 978-1-62979-440-2 • Library of Congress Control Number: 2018962345

First edition
10 9 8 7 6 5 4 3 2 1

Design by Barbara Grzeslo • The text is set in Futura Book. • The artwork is done in mixed media and digital.